Gathering Silence

Sayings by Ivan M. Granger

Collages by Rashani Réa

POETRY CHAIKHANA

www.poetry-chaikhana.com

ISBN: 0-9854679-6-7
ISBN-13: 978-0-9854679-6-8

To Ken,

who showed me how to live
with kindness, heart, humor,
and index cards.

Introduction

I inherited my love of quotes and aphorisms from my grandfather. I particularly remember one Christmas at my grandparents' house as a child when I was playing with my grandfather's roll-top desk. I was fascinated by the way the wooden slats rolled up and down along their grooved curving path. That's when I discovered a small box tucked away in the desk. Opening it, I found dozens of index cards, each with just a sentence or two written in my grandfather's neat hand. He had been collecting favorite quotes, jokes, even overheard snippets of conversation. This felt like a magical window into the private thoughts of a man I loved and idolized.

I began to keep index cards with me, usually half-bent in my pocket, ready any time I wanted to write down a random thought, lines from a novel, an uplifting quote, or a half-remembered dream. I still do it today. I keep stacks of index cards strategically placed throughout the house.

Sometimes in meditation a thought or insight will pop into my head, fully formed in the silence. It immediately gets scribbled onto an index card to sit on my desk or nightstand, so it can be reread and contemplated. These sayings speak to me as much as for me.

And that's the interesting thing about my relationship with the sayings gathered in this book. I wrote them, but they still surprise me. Sometimes I feel that I found them rather than formulated them. Am I their author or simply a transcriber? In my lucid moments, they are my words, my voice. But they are also the guidance I turn to when life's burdens weigh heavily and the spiritual path seems unclear. It is as if a larger self is leaving helpful notes to a sometimes struggling smaller self.

In that spirit I present these sayings, as both author and audience. I hope you find that they guide and illuminate, prod and awaken, as they continue to do for me. And perhaps they will even speak to you in your own voice.

These sayings are intentionally kept to just one or two per page in most cases, allowing each page to become a restful mental space for contemplation and inspiration. This is not a book to be rushed through. And while there is a thematic progression through the book, it is not necessarily meant to be read front to back.

When you have a question or a quiet moment, pick this book up, flip to a random page, and spend some time with the few words you discover there. You may want to read the words aloud or quietly repeat them to yourself. Even if the words don't immediately make sense, sit with them, and see what sense you can make of them. Play with the words and the meaning.

Let them ferment and dance beneath your thoughts.
Then wait and watch what rises to the surface.

The best sayings inspire the same silence from which
they emerged. That's what I hope for you as you read
these pages, the discovery of words that disappear
into silence, drawing you in after them.

I want to especially thank Rashani Réa for the
stunning collages she has contributed to this book.
With their rich colors, organic forms, and fluid lines,
her collages feel as if they have been grown in a secret
magical garden. Her artwork is alive, glowing with an
inner light. Letting one's eyes meander through the
interplay of colors and textures in her collages
becomes a rich meditation in itself. I couldn't be more
pleased to have my words illuminated by Rashani's
creative touch.

Ivan M. Granger
December 2016

Ask yourself:

Are you one who seeks,
or one who finds?

Decide on a goal.

Then make the road
to that goal
your daily practice.

Let your longing
lead you.

THE PARCHED KNOW~

real THIRST
DRAWS RAINWATER
FROM AN EMPTY SKY.

All the world
is an altar.

In every corner of the world,
the entire mystery of life and death
can be found.

Through you
the world learns
to recognize itself
— as heaven.

The purpose of spiritual practice
is to intelligently strain your system
while giving your awareness the courage
to leap into silence.

—∽—

A mystic must be supremely pragmatic:

Use what works,
whatever opens the heart
and fires the spirit.

ALL OF MYSTICISM COMES DOWN TO THIS:

TO RECOGNIZE
WHAT IS ALREADY
AND ALWAYS HERE.

We become what we love.

Everything else is just movement.

Each life
is a grand philosophical experiment
within unfathomable mystery.

Curiosity, wonder—uncertainty,
these give us eyes.

Questions awaken the soul.

Whittle yourself down

to the question at your core.

Let that empty ache
lead you to ecstasy!

GRACE IS WHAT OCCURS
WHEN WE STOP OBSTRUCTING
THAT NATURAL PROCESS.

Regardless of belief,

everyone is agnostic
until gnosis.

Dogma is for those
who have tired
      of the search.

⁎

When you know where the Beloved lives,
you are content,
      no need to argue with others
      over street names.

Religion that does not inspire
        outward compassion
        and inward awakening
is not religion.

—ɯ—

No one gets to heaven
        by following the rules
        —or breaking them.

Heaven must burst forth from your breast.

The theologian
reformulates other people's
descriptions of sugar and tells
himself that he is content.

But the mystic is only satisfied
with tasting the sweetness.

About sacred texts:

A map doesn't mean much
if you don't make the journey.

Meditation is not what you do,
it is what you are.

A courageous prayer:

God, use me
       any way you want
       for the healing of the world.

Approach the trysting place
naked.

If you come any other way,
what's the point?

Call out to be grabbed whole.

Every person: God.

Every animal, every plant: God.

Everything: God, God!

The slightest contact is worship.

BELOVED, THEY WANT TO KNOW:
DID I REACH UP TO YOU,
OR DID YOU REACH OUT TO ME?

AND THEY WANT TO KNOW:
WHAT IS REAL
TOUCH?

HOW
CAN I
EXPLAIN

-- WE POUR
INTO EACH OTHER.

Love and compassion are effortless.

The soul is exhausted by its effort
to stop the natural outpouring
of the living heart.

All that loss, hurt and hope—
     gather them up
     into a great pure ache

until the Beloved has no choice but to kiss
     your naked heart.

There
is no letting
go.

Even your absence touches me.
The new moon is not gone;
she hides her face
in the night.

Our wounds
are the marks of initiation.

Our wounds
are our wisdom.

Our wounds tell the story
of our journey.

—ɯ—

Even through intense suffering
the Divine is revealed
—exquisitely!

YOUR MOST SECRET WOUND
IS THE DOORWAY.

Even our tragedies are filled
with blessings.

—⊱

There is a perverse sort of blessing
that comes from calamity:

We might just give ourselves permission
to surrender.

LET THE VISION
OF THE VASTNESS YOU ARE

LEAVE YOU IN GLORIOUS RUINS.

Enough deals and half-measures!

Hand everything over
        to that divine ember
        burning in your chest!

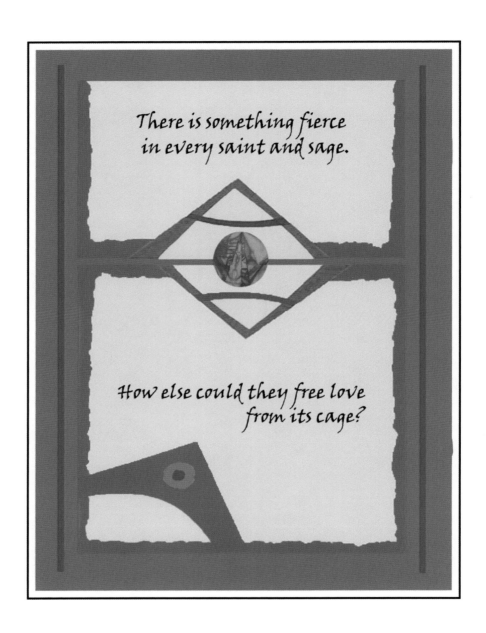

There is something fierce
in every saint and sage.

How else could they free love
from its cage?

In this divine game of hide-and-seek
stop pretending
there is any place to hide.

Outwardly, determined effort is necessary.

But within, nothing is needed
except to yield.

Protect
the wild places
in yourself.

Seek those moments
when you gently come to a stop.

Stay there.

SOME DAYS IT'S BEST
TO DO NOTHING
BUT RING LIKE A TAPPED BELL.

Each step
is part of the journey.

Accept every step
that has led you here.

The pathway
runs along the seam
between the heart and the world.

Awakening
requires a tremendous journey,

but nothing much
needs to happen.

Maybe the journey's end
is just around the corner.

Maybe it is right under your feet.

﹏

Any step
—done well—
completes the journey.

We can spend a lifetime
looking, traveling, and acquiring.
Or we can look in the mirror.

Forget about what should be.
Discover what is.

The greatest teacher
    is what is
immediately in front of you.

Inhabit each raw minute.

EACH DAY, EACH MOMENT
IS A STEP INTO THE UNKNOWN.
HOW CAN WE FEEL ANYTHING
BUT AMAZEMENT?

Where you are,
worship.

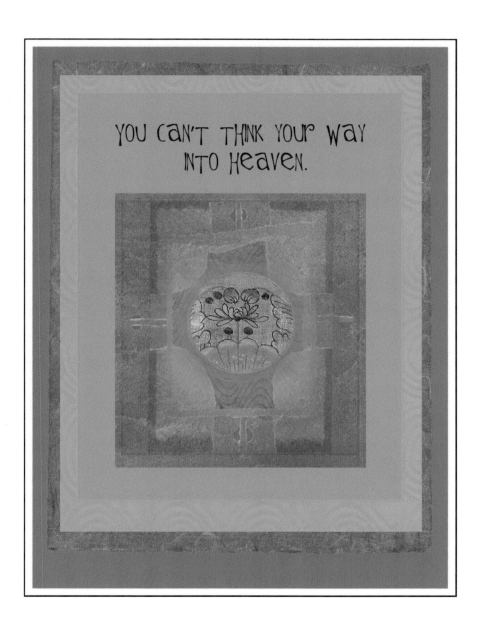

YOU CAN'T THINK YOUR WAY
INTO HEAVEN.

God inhabits the space

between our thoughts.

see
everything
with a fierce eye
and a gentle heart.

You can only perceive
what you already are.

Allow yourself to notice
      what you are feeling.
Then—notice yourself feeling.
Then—notice yourself.

_᠗

When awareness rests,
      it recognizes itself.

THE INDIVIDUAL IS REALLY
A MAGICAL ACT OF SEEING
WITH NO FIXED EYE.

Everything is an exercise
in awareness.

The mind, in its stillness,
in recognizing its nothingness,
manages to reflect
the immensity of eternity.

The agitations of the mind
are addictive.

Break that addiction
and see what the still mind sees.

Finally, we fall silent.

Finally, we witness ourselves as we are.

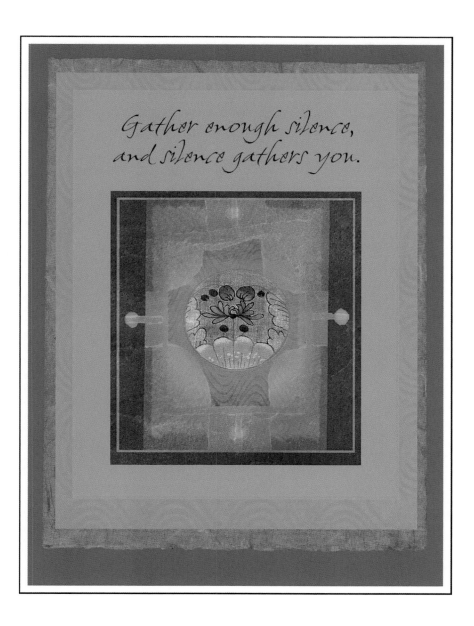

Gather enough silence,
and silence gathers you.

The ego is a personal myth,
      a story we tell ourselves
     about who we are.

That story can change, expand,
          or fall silent.

What we call the ego
is the individual's particular way
of not being fully present.

The goal for the ego is not perfection.

Its ultimate goal is to fade away
in order to reveal
the inherent perfection
already present.

You are a gauze-like veil
draped over the Divine.

The slightest puff of breath
            or flaming spark
dispels the illusion of substance.

How can you settle into yourself
without
self-acceptance?

—◊—

Accept yourself
so deeply
that you are not afraid to let go
of what is not you.

—◊—

Self-acceptance
mysteriously becomes
self-awareness.

And what is the Buddha's body but us?
The Buddha's body is our very nature.

That Mystery
devastating in its immensity,
it whispers:

"I am your very self."

We are the flash of self-recognition
that lights the face of the Divine.

Too tired to maintain our pretenses,

we rest in awe.

The holiest place
we can discover

is immediately behind the breastbone.

⌒

The awakened heart
is the true church.

Find the joy
that quietly glows in your chest,

the joy that glows
with brazen disregard
for your tears and laughter.

Somehow the battered heart
blossoms with such beauty,
no hint of past hurts.

The Divine is experienced by the heart.

The intellect, at best, can only trail behind
and take notes.

What the heart recognizes
as liberation,
　　　the ego sees
　　　as theft.

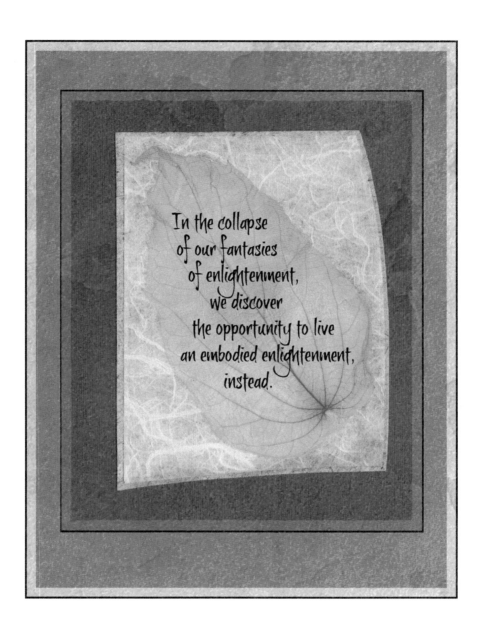

In the collapse
of our fantasies
of enlightenment,
we discover
the opportunity to live
an embodied enlightenment,
instead.

Don't strain toward enlightenment.
Relax into it.

See—

you are
a lamp
lost in light.

Enlightenment all the way to enlightenment.

(Remember:

Rogues too realize.)

When that final door opens,
       does it really matter
   how long you waited?

We don't take the final step.

It takes us.

Read these words, but ignore them.
The silence will teach you.

About the Author

Ivan M. Granger is a poet and modern mystic. He grew up in Oregon and California, and lived for several years in retreat in Hawaii and Colorado. Ivan is the founder and editor of the *Poetry Chaikhana*, a publishing house and online resource for sacred poetry from around the world. He is the author of *Real Thirst: Poetry of the Spiritual Journey* and editor of *The Longing in Between: A Poetry Chaikhana Anthology*. His poetry and translations have been included in several magazines and anthologies.

> *"Poetry has an immediate effect on the mind. The simple act of reading poetry alters thought patterns and the shuttle of the breath. Poetry induces trance. Its words are chant. Its rhythms are drumbeats. Its images become the icons of the inner eye. Poetry is more than a description of the sacred experience; it carries the experience itself."*

www.poetry-chaikhana.com

About the Artist

A prolific artist, intimist, and social activist since childhood, **Rashani Réa** has designed hundreds of collages, incorporating words from a diverse selection of writers, mystics, poets, woman identified women, holy rebels, teachers, and spiritual pioneers. During the past 25 years she has co-created two Dharma-Gaia sanctuaries on the Big Island of Hawaii, where she currently lives.

She offers councils, concerts, kirtans, and retreats throughout the world and at her home, Kipukamaluhia Sanctuary, in Ka'u. She is also a mother, an earth steward, and tree planter. A published poet at the age of 12, Rashani is the creatrix of several books and has recorded 15 albums of devotional chants and Soetry (songs and poetry.)

www.rashani.com

64888756R00052

Made in the USA
Charleston, SC
10 December 2016